Wishful Thinking

New and Collected Poems

Nathan Polsky

Volume 4

Copyright © 2015 by Nathan Polsky
All rights reserved. No part of this book may be reproduced, scanned, or distributed in any printed or electronic form without permission.
First Edition: June 2015
Printed in the United States of America
ISBN: 978-1-939237-38-5

Cover Art
"Autumn Color Blocks" by Debbie Dannheisser

To Janet

Foreword

Nathan Polsky is doing just what I want to do:
writing good poetry at age 92!

Nathan Polsky, in this collection (fourth in the series of his published volumes of poetry), shares some of his inspirational mind-set. One example from this book, WISHFUL THINKING, is found in his poem *Search and Find*:

> *So, "Come out, come out; wherever you're hiding!"*
> *I'll never stop playing that game!*
> *I'll never stop searching for meaning and goals.*
> *If smart, you'll do the same!*

Instead of reviewing illnesses, Polsky keeps himself youthful in the company of his muse. He finds himself so often reviewing words and phrases, a rhyme that needs work, and with "thoughts in overdrive," as he shares in another poem, *Out of Sync*:

> *As I lay me down to sleep,*
> *my brain is still alive.*
> *I cannot stop my speeding train:*
> *my thoughts are in over-drive!*

Poetry matters intensely to some. Readers will relate to Polsky's disarming honesty about self-reflection, growing old, and the way poetry bridges the present and past.

This following poem, Balance, brilliantly captures the hard-earned wisdom and satisfaction of the artist at work:

> *It's such a joy to be wrapped*
> *in a blanket of private silence,*
> *so solitude can water the dormant seeds*
> *of a poem, or any artistic activity.*

*The trick with such self-absorption
is maintaining a realistic and harmonious
balance with marital
and other social relationships,
extending beyond one's self.*

*Such deliberate withdrawal
demands a social price —
whatever the resulting product
or one's simple recharge.*

Poetry keeps us engaged. Poetry, to me, is a special game for grown-up people. Poetry helps us know what we think, and to recognize kindred hearts sharing wisdom and memories.

Bravo *WISHFUL THINKING,* as I look forward to more poetry!

—Jo Ann Lordahl, Ph.D.

Author, poet, speaker

www.joannlordahl.com

Author's Note

I'm delighted to offer Vol. 4, *WISHFUL THINKING*, to add to my previous three volumes:

> Vol. 1– *MEANINGFUL SOUNDS*
> Vol. 2 – *BOUNTIFUL BUFFET*
> Vol. 3 – *TRAVELING LIGHT*

A mind is filled with memories, observations, criticisms and the occasional ingisht that is one of the remaining fruits of advancing age.

Most of these poems are written following simple rhyming tradition with occasional lapses into free verse or commentary.

Share with me the comedic, philosophical, thought-provoking, escapist and musing that this book offers.

Nathan Polsky

Contents

Foreword	VII
Author's Note	IX
A Hurtful First	1
A Moment In Time	2
Bubble	3
Awaited News	4
Just Asking	5
Resolution	6
Melancholy Summary	7
Sonya, The Wise	8
Tipping Is Optional	9
Impressed	10
Transition	11
Always Thinking.:	12
Puzzling Questions	14
Identity	15
Wishful Thinking	16
Observation	17
Search And Find	18
Timeless	19
Cycle	20
Destiny	21
Portrait	22
Out Of Sync	23
Silent Language	24
Lost Vintage	26
A Message: Old And New	28
Body Language	29
Retribution	30
Neighborly	31
Our Face	32
Anticipation	34
Simple Truth	35
Public Domain	36
Envy	38
Political Realities	39

CALENDAR TID-BITS	40
A LIKELY STORY	42
PULP IDOL	43
GRATITUDE	44
CURIOUS	46
CONSUMED	48
PLAYTIME	49
DEVIL'S GARDEN	50
REVEALED!	51
CHARISMA	52
VALENTINE POEM	53
WITNESS	54
NASAL RECALL	55
FRONTAL CRUDITY	56
READ ALL ABOUT IT!	57
HARVEST	58
TAKING THE SUN	59
BUSINESS OF LIFE	60
WILD RIDE	61
ALL IS NOT LOST	62
SURPRISING ENCOUNTERS	63
ATTUNED	64
A GRALLO'S TLO	65
WHERE I DRAW THE LINE!	66
THE PENDULUM'S ARC	67
TOGETHERNESS	68
REMEMBERING	70
THAT OLD PHILCO AND EMERSON	72
OVERDOSE	73
PICTORIAL	74
ADRIFT	75
JUST WONDERING	76
A HOPELESS WISH	77
MENDERS	78
HELPFUL ID	79
A NARCISSIST'S POEM	80
NATURE'S PAYBACK	81
HOLLYWOOD PREVIEW	82
ADIEU!	83

Song Of The Vernacular	84
Dark Matter	85
Be Gone!	86
Memorable Moment	87
Good Morning	88
Collective Loss	89
Short Story	90
Challenge	91
Basic Training	92
The Last Word	95
Keeping Informed	96
Renewal	97
Choices	98
Hat Chat	99
Balance	100
Dark Thoughts	101
Persuasion	102
Shower	103
Sales Pitch	104
Mate Search	105
Image	106
Delicious Memories	107
HA-HA-HA	108
A Bright Idea!	109
Free To Fail	110
An Uncomfortable Truth	111
Bottled Poetry: What A Copywriter Might Write!	112
You're Wasting Your Time	113
Wishes	114
String Theory	115
Forgotten	116
Archive	117
Problems Solved	118
Still More Rambling	119
Intertwined	120
A Toast	122
Final Chores	123
About The Author	125
Previously Published By Nathan Polsky	127

A Hurtful First

I'll never forget the first time it happened,
when someone gave her seat to me.
The bus was crowded as I entered to ride,
and I expected no favors for free.

I was very embarrassed and tried to decline,
but, she obviously thought I would fall.
To this day I've wondered what she had seen,
(I always thought I was handsome and tall).

But, there's always a first time along our life's road:
those things we cannot forget;
like the day when a kid's shorts gave way to long pants,
a first friend, first kiss, and first pet.

That first birthday cake, that first day in school,
the diploma and attention received;
the first intimate touch; first job and its pay:
it seemed like so much achieved.

Then, sweethearts and marriage, and baby's first steps.
Life consisted of lots we call "first!",
But, I'm not ready to accept that girl giving her seat!
Oh, if she only knew how many bubbles she burst!

A Moment In Time

The water runs in a constant stream,
in puddling, eddying flow.
From whence to where is a puzzle to me,
for this moment, it's not mine to know

The sun reflects on its rippling course,
a vein in a woodsy, green calm;
providing rides to visiting leaves:
it's such a visual, delightful balm!

An occasional silvery fish waves "Hello!",
accenting such a painter's tableau.
A cityscape offers what man can do best,
but, a soul needs nature to grow!

A steadfast rock in the current's midst
plays host to gossiping birds.
Thus transfixed by such sight and sounds,
what poet can select adequate words?

Bubble

This moment is my armored shield,
the touch and breath called now:
that centered self, my island home,
escaping how or Dow.

All foreign noise and pressing ills
are beyond my respite's needs.
My garden's core, the flowery peace,
won't tolerate any weeds.

My psychic eyes shut out the dross,
as inward quiet reigns.
I'm of this world and yet aside,
where solace soothes the pains.

Problem's broth is kept at bay,
as stranger to my core.
I defy its cries and siren's beck:
the need is to ignore!

Surrendering, thus, to serenity,
escaping stress's toll,
I can return again greatly fortified,
with rejuvenated soul.

Awaited News

Every day brings breakthrough news
of our genetic and basic selves,
filling knowledge voids
and explaining drives and traits.

I await the discovery of the male wheel gene.

Just Asking

I don't know why some say "I know not",
and leaving becomes "I'm off!";
or dying is to "kick the bucket"
or lifting one's hat is "doff"?

To share the news, I become a chef
when friends all ask "What's cooking?"
When wandering in a department store,
I innocently say "Just looking".

Why are liquored people "high",
and some folks feel so "low"?
Why is not eating called a "fast"?
And why are some wits slow?

When something's easy to accomplish,
why say "It's a breeze"?
Please explain why "mum's the word"?
And why do cops say "Freeze!"?

When someone says "You said a mouthful!"
how could they have been clearly heard?
Why don't we respect the iconoclast more
who refuses to "follow the herd"?

When you understand what I have to say,
you say "I get the drift!".
And when someone offers you a ride,
why is it called a "lift"?

Why's taking a chance "sticking your neck out"?
Do you really "smell a rat" when suspicious?
Why is some news "hard to swallow"?
Is all food for thought delicious?

Resolution

I must go down to the gym today,
but, the temptation to lie around wins.
I look at my neighbors' fancy gym duds,
knowing laziness adds to my sins.

They run on the treadmill, never showing a sweat
(that thing in their ear jogging, too!).
Endlessly pounding, their sneakers don't rest:
bottled water is their favorite brew.

I enviously watch as they lift and they push:
each machine speaks a language they know.
Their muscles seem to grow as mine shrink.
Can my ego take such a blow?

Tomorrow I'll start, I ernestly promise:
there's going to be a new me!
I'll lose those pounds and push gray hairs aside.
Don't laugh! Just you wait and see!

Melancholy Summary

It's really quite simple: we're just passing through.
We learn, we love, procreate.
Some days are sunny, some damp and dark.
Our visit ends sooner or late!

We're not invincible, master of life:
at the end, some bodies are frail.
Others are suddenly called at God's whim.
Be objective, and learn from this tale.

No promises were made or guarantees given.
We work hard and hope for the best.
Along the way we make some good friends,
with a loving mate, kids and a nest.

We play, we cry, disappointments abound.
We clutch at serenity and peace.
Our few years allowed is God's gift to us:
until all memories cease!

We survive in the minds of those left behind:
memories, as we cherished ours,
Our residue left returns to the earth,
or in air, or possibly flowers.

Sonya, The Wise

Her name was Sonya, the printed ad said,
and I smiled as I read what she did.
Her self-described talents were hard to believe,
for she could reveal whatever was hid.

I've read many ads that promised a lot,
but, I'll never forget this one.
It brought a chuckle and a raised brow;
or was someone just having fun?

The ad was about Sonya, a spiritual healer,
a helpful advisor to all.
The first reading would be free on the phone,
and it listed a number to call.

She'll know the causes of problems without asking,
and with advice to solve every one!
She'll reveal the names of enemies and friends,
and suggest how inner peace is won.

She can re-unite lovers or stop a divorce,
help childless couples conceive.
If Sonya cannot help you, no one else can:
her advice is the best you'll receive!

She'll bring success to your business, better your job,
heal sickness with her spiritual way.
I was tempted to call, but wisdom prevailed:
I was very impressed, I must say!

She can help you with curses, witchcraft and voodoo,
dispel evil spirits and spells;
eliminate depression, help pass exams:
protect you from disasters and hells!

I was also puzzled, that with powers like these,
why can't she improve her own lot?
Now, do I believe in such profound gifts?
Do you believe I'm stupid, or what?

Tipping Is Optional

It's a dangerous diner which nature provides,
everything is eating or eaten.
Wherever you look, whatever the time,
someone's a victor or beaten.

No niceties exist like knives, spoons or forks:
more useful are teeth and sharp claws.
No animal is known to lift a pinky when dining:
relying, instead, on strong jaws.

To grow and to thrive on our singular planet
depends on weapons and tricks.
It's a perpetual game of offense and defense;
even mosquitoes don't suck blood for kicks!

There are poisons and toxins, odors and quills,
camouflage, speed and disguise.
It's a game of finding or avoiding being food:
with growing and thriving the prize:

So, from appetizer to entrée, ending up with dessert,
napkins are not needed here.
The difference between us and what's in the wild,
is we eat with some wine or a cold beer!

We pay others to hunt, to fish and to farm;
we've conquered the need for our food.
We've made eating more delicious, available and cheap:
whether baked, fried, roasted or stewed:

IMPRESSED

Last night I watched a TV show,
an orangutan was the star.
It had such an intelligent look in its eyes,
the experience was bizarre!

It was finding objects and opening locks,
and was smarter than any baby I knew!
It responded and did whatever was asked.
How it did it, I haven't a clue!

It counted and did some other great tricks:
even responding to finger signs.
I appreciated evolution even more than I did,
for, I could imagine us swinging on vines!

With a little more time, its future is clear:
I can see it with jacket and tie.
It would ask for my money to invest in some stock,
or become a skate-boarding guy!

TRANSITION

When leaves say good-bye to branches and limbs
and signal the waning year:
When temperatures fall and sharp, breezes felt,
a desire for change becomes clear!

When days become shorter and windy and cold,
and the winter play curtain ascends;
and out come the mufflers, hats and the gloves,
then, it's time to rejoin southern friends!

We attend to the ritual of forwarding mail,
and suspend the phone and TV;
and clearly the birds, in purposeful flight,
becken and say "Follow me!".

I just don't like ice and chattering teeth:
and I'm getting too old for snow.
So, as much as I love scenes of chimney smoke,
I prefer Santa's beach ball's "HO! HO!"!

Always Thinking.:

Doodads, gadgets, what-nots or gimmicks,
each adds convenience to our lives.
Those little things that ease our way,
like paper clips or sharpening knives.

Stamps that stick, can openers, too;
convenient coffee maker,
orange squeezer, flat-top tacks,
erasable slate, clock waker.

Battery tooth brush, a sponge that wipes,
glue sticks and cans that spray;
convenient packets of sugar and cream,
GPS to help find the way.

Heating pads, windshield wipers,
transparent tape was once new;
rheostat dimmer for the light,
and Band-Aids for the boo-boo!

There's white-out for the writer's mistake,
re-tractable measuring tape;
mirrors that magnify and don't lie,
treadmills to help keep in shape!

Who thought of tissues in boxes and rolls,
safety pins or the shoe horn?
We should be grateful for whoever thought of these;
and those two little holders for corn!

Steel wool for the pots, combs for the hair,
napkins when eating are handy.
We all need a calendar to remember
and a calculator that adds is dandy.

The list can go on just by looking around:
man is so ingenious and clever!
Should we believe that's the end of our gizmos?
Our love for convenience says "Never!"

Simple and clever devices keep coming,
thanks to those tinkerers and nerds.
And as I sit here and muse under this tree,
I await someone's diaper for birds.

Puzzling Questions

Why do stars twinkle and smoke always rises,
or clouds form their fluffier shapes?
And why does it seem that when sunsets occur,
it's like nature drawing shut its drapes?

Why do squirrels have puffy, curved tails,
and are considered so picturesque and cute?
We love to see their scampering and poses,
and wish they weren't so mute!

Why are some pits so rock-like and hard,
yet soften and sprout and bloom?
And if there are two words we should never have to use,
they probably are "gloom" and "doom".

Why does one say "cute as a button"?
Why is a not-nice man a "heel"?
Why do they say "Keep your shirt on!"?
Is something you cannot see "real"?

Is each leg a "pant" when we say a pair of pants?
Why is somebody's story a "yarn"?
And when we hit a finger with a hammer,
how many of us would just say "Darn!"?

Does a fish ever graduate from its school?
Will there ever be a Wal-mart on Mars?
Why is luck a "Lady" and a door is a jar?
Are czardines the children of Czars?

IDENTITY

Girls, surely are our flowerly half,
as favored by a name.
A look at lists of garden's growth
supports this little game.

There's Iris, Lily, Violet, Rose,
Jasmine, Daisy, Fern;
Hyacinth, Blossom and there's Rhoda,
I was surprised to learn.

There's Tulip,. Orchid and, also, Ivy;
Camellia, Gardenia, Holly.
Also, Laurel, Heather, Ginger,
(This poem is fun, by golly!).

I've heard of Dahlia and of Lilac,
and Susan with eyes of black.
My tired brain suggests I stop:
it's too tired to further rack!

When boys are hatched and must be named,
the garden's not for them.
More virile names would be the choice:
like Zachary or Clem!

Wishful Thinking

OK! OK! I ask you now,
who took my youth away?
What must I do and whom to ask,
to keep old age at bay?

Where is that potion, pill or med
to make my sinews strong?
What jar of magic, juice or prayer
can bring back youth and song?

Someday eternal youth may come,
too late. of course, for me:
with parts and brains from off the shelf,
and kinder mirrors that see.

Until such time I'll take what's here,
and know it could be worse.
I'll try to keep a happy smile
and confine my thoughts to verse.

Observation

Seven thousand dollar purses,
300,000 dollar cars,
two thousand dollars for a pair of shoes,
and more for a reserved trip to Mars!

Three thousand dollars for a suit,
(whatever happened to spats?).
Our economy now provides ground middle-class
in cans for our hungry Fat Cats!

Search And Find

"Come out, come out wherever you are!"
I loved that game we played!
I'd count to ten while others hid:
instincts our only aid.

We pit our wits in hide and seek,
and tested our logic and skill.
The one thus found was then the seeker,
until we had our fill!

That game that now sounds so very simple
was a challenge as it brought friends together.
Our playing field could be anywhere
and, indoors, ignored the weather!

But, it's also a critical real-life need,
for our elusive dreams are hiding,
awaiting discovery with optimistic hope,
with persistence and good Fate's guiding!

So, "Come out, come out; wherever you're hiding!"
I'll never stop playing that game!
I'll never stop searching for meaning and goals.
If smart, you'll do the same!

Timeless

She stares at me, but sees me not;
her gaze looks through my own.
Her lips are small with trace of smile,
with thoughts as if alone.

Her hair is swept back into a bun,
with untucked strands behind:
a simple bow, a string of pearls;
the sculptor's touch was kind.

Thus frozen in her marble white,
the face will never age.
Her future viewers will share her youth:
for she's escaped our mortal cage.

Cycle

Those aging leaves have lost their grip,
and fall silently to earth,
providing a crispy, rustling coat
three seasons from their birth.

They've had their share of nature's food,
while offering shade and home;
umbilical stems once anchored firm
supply image for this poem.

From youthful greens to golds and reds,
leaves had their glory days.
I, too, detect my weakening stem:
earth-bound in similar ways.

Destiny

While walking down a city street,
I saw a window sign
that promised to tell the future to be:
so I decided to discover mine.

The light was dim, I was asked to sit,
then this kerchiefed woman spoke.
She said I was born as royalty:
I wasn't just common folk!

She took my palm, then stood up straight,
and said I'd be filthy rich;
I'd travel all around the globe,
until I found my niche.

She laid out cards, and her eyes lit up,
for she saw my changed luck clearly.
She said I'd inherit a beach-front lot.
All I could say was "Really?".

Next, she studied her crystal ball,
which revealed her final word.
She said that somehow nature erred,
for I was meant to be a bird!

On my way home, I heard a bird tweet,
as I passed beneath a tree.
I forgot the wealth and royal births—
Golly! That could've been me!

Portrait

An image recurs, when least expected,
Of my grandfather, my father's father,
who, in my youth, appeared as a distantly
strange figure with a gray, short stubbly beard,
tobacco stained, with its accompanying odor.

He came with his wife, my grandmother,
from Russia as one of those countless immigrants
(seeking opportunity? change? escape from oppression?)
accompanied by his four children:
my father and his three brothers and sister,
my aunt, in whose home he boarded.

My earliest recollection of him
was as a tall, no-nonsense fellow
who enjoyed two home-brewed specialties:
a liquor resulting from fermented mysterious ingredients,
and sour pickles with their briny juice.
Whenever I recall visiting him,
he was partaking of one or the other.

He tried to contribute his bit for his board
by selling large, soft, salted pretzels,
(tasting so memorably good when he offered one to me)
stacked on vertical sticks anchored to a
rectangular woven wooden basket,
behind which he sat on an upended box.

The figure of him sitting patiently there,
wearing his black derby hat in front of a movie house
is an image hard to erase, to this day.

Our pasts are riddled with such tantalizing tid-bits,
ghostly hints, contributing to the flavor
of our remembered history.

In the future, when my own grandchildren
think of their grandfather, or grandmother,
I wonder what special event, scene or image
will be recalled to *their* minds.

Out Of Sync

As I lay me down to sleep,
my brain is still alive.
I cannot stop my speeding train:
my thoughts are in over-drive!

The poem I started and laid aside,
half-done and needing a rhyme,
in sleepless stupor I struggle still,
knowing it's a bodily crime!

I know it's not the proper place:
a bed is made for sleep.
The desk or pad can await my day:
life's more than counting sheep!

And, so, the bedside clock mocks me,
I sit up and mutter curses.
I really should be soundly sleeping,
and not reviewing verses!

Silent Language

Our hand is a great conversational tool;
our fingers speak a language we know.
They deserve a moment or two of our thought,
for they can say "Come hither!" or "Go!"

The thumb asks for rides, and when raised says "I approve!",
And, of course, thumb to nose is quite clear.
We all welcome and appreciate the pat on the back!
A threatening raised fist we all fear!

A cupped palm makes a great hearing aid;
a forefinger to lips asks for quiet.
Forming a circle means "I approve!" and "It's great!"
A push from the table helps a diet!

A pointed finger can identify and accuse.
When raised, the fan's team is number one!
A middle finger's message is an insult well-known;
Pointed finger and raised thumb is a gun!

The Boy Scout makes a two-finger pledge;
five fingers to cap is a salute!
Success includes a mutual "high five".
Circling thumb to finger means "a beaut!"

Two clapping palms show appreciation and response.
A cop's raised hand means "STOP!"
Rome's Caesar decided with thumb up or down!
And we know about the karate chop!

Two touching palms can be raised in prayer;
a wagging finger is upsetting!
Two raised wide fingers is a victory sign.
A dog would appreciate petting.

A violinist's fingers are impressive when playing.
A ring is the vow that we make.
An umpire's palms down means safe at the plate;
we say "Hello!" and "Good-bye!" with a shake!

But the ultimate communication skill that we know
is seen when sign language is used.
It provides silent "ears" replacing the verbal.
where meaning and fingers are fused!

Lost Vintage

The 2-story house stood proudly alone,
the sideboards were gray with age:
exposed to infinite seasons of rain and snow.
heat and freeze, blizzard and gales:
a proud vestige of honest carpentry.

The rooms were spacious with wide wooden flooring,
heated with cordwood in a central hearth,
that brought seasonal comfort and pleasure.

The house was a classical picture-postcard,
rustic, colonial dwelling, with a reading-friendly
back porch, the immediate destination upon arrival.

Our house enjoyed its companionship
with its surrounding towering pines,
and sat almost at the edge of a large lake,
with views of sailboats and canoes in summer,
and, in winter, intrepid, patient,
well-insulated fishermen holding fish-shopping
lines, dropped into holes bored through
the floor of frozen ice.

In winter months, with snow-covered paths,
cross-country skiing compounded the value
of our hide-away gem!

Then, disaster struck!

We were notified that our lovely home
had been destroyed by a fire!
Our serene, private country retreat was gone!

It seems that several home fires occurred in the area,
and the first responder reporting the fire,
was a local police officer, the suspected offender,
always the first at the scenes.

He was accused and brought to trial,
but, no viable evidence, except the circumstantial,
could prove the case!

He was acquitted and hurriedly left town!
But, our picture-perfect dream cottage was gone!

We re-built, with a more modern structure,
but it lacked history, flavor, innocence and charm!
The mystique was gone! Memories will have to suffice.

A Message: Old And New

You must believe what I believe
or I will kill you. Or stone you.
Or whip you until you admit
that what I believe is more valid,
more truthful than what you, mistakenly, believe.

If you depart or seek to forego,
or become entwined, with another's beliefs,
you will be endangered,
and suffer the pain of your mis-step.

Only my own and divine and holy
Allah, God, Saint, Redeemer, Creator, Father
is the true possessor of all power,
deserving of worship and prayer,
sacrifice and adulation.

All others are shams, and destroyers
of true faith, and their followers
are apostates, dangerous, undeserving of sympathy,
and, as unbelievers, subject to punishment
or death and unworthy of life.

My Almighty has been given to me
by His true and only earthly messenger,
through whose grace, memory, person, and divinity,
homage is paid to the Divine and Holy One.
Also given are specific, sanctified words,
practices and rituals, with the hope of joining HIM
one day in eternal bliss, comfort and plenty.

There cannot be any other belief or practice,
other than such commandments
on pain of torture or death.
Your head and body will bow with mine
and my brother believers.
For only we are the selected possessors of the TRUTH!

Peace be with you.

Body Language

They dance, they prance, arms waving in arcs.
They leap and twist and twirl!
Such energy raw embarrasses me,
for my own body's unable to whirl!

They fling each other like sacks of grain;
they jump in entangled pairs.
They contort without ever saying a word:
and they buck like unbroken mares!

The stage timbers heave, and recall, I am sure,
those tu-tu-ed dancers so regal:
whose classic pirouettes and pliés are familiar:
what's danced now some think is illegal!

Street dancers now get close to the ground,
and swivel and kick up their heels.
No music need play for there are no rules:
one moves however one feels!

Tradition shares space with contemporary dance;
it's fun to see what the young do.
it's a great energy outlet for personal expression.
What's next? We haven't a clue!

Formally scripted or compulsively improvised,
it's a language of "body-speak":
ballroom, folk, tap or new craze,
without dance, life itself would be bleak!

Retribution

While playing during a summer season farm vacation,
another city boy trampled
on my carefully constructed
miniature house and barn,
made of earth and twigs,
and ran away to avoid my wrath.

Angered, I picked up a fallen crab apple,
took aim, computed wind velocity
and trajectory angle,
and threw my projectile to that point
ahead of him where I thought he'd be
on impact.

It was a perfect throw!
It was a satisfying retribution!
And an early indicator of my future role
as Air Force Bombardier!

Neighborly

I love to watch a city pigeon walk
with its pendulum back-and-forth neck.
Its eyes must be sharp whenever it dines,
for it picks up the tiniest speck!

If one should happen to be lucky and find
some stray seeds or crumbs on the ground,
it's so delightful to hear that song of success:
a contented and cooing sound.

Successfully finding its morsel or snack,
there's suddenly a flurry of wings,
as others want a share of the find:
it's the price that sweet success brings.

What's also amusing is the tolerant patience,
and to see those little sparrows get theirs.
Everyone is busily engaged in their search,
and not one of the big boys cares!

Such open-air dining brings smiles at the antics:
the pigeons walking like us;
while the sparrows prefer hopping, both feet together,
friendly and tolerant, without fuss!

Our Face

Let's consider our face for a moment or two
and see how it serves us so well;
its nuances and expressions is the mask we show,
the house behind which we dwell.

We're sullen or bewildered, blushing or smiling,
frowning or wrinkling our nose,
furrowing our brow, winking or sad,
or shutting our eyes when we doze.

We grin and blow kisses and give dirty looks,
and sometimes we steal a glance;
we're down in the mouth, but keep a stiff upper lip;
we also question and look askance.

We scowl, raise an eyebrow and nod our approval,
thumb our nose or stick our tongue out,
and roll our eyes in disbelief:
we're downcast, glaring and pout.

Our nostrils can flare when angry or mad;
they say we turn purple with rage,
or green with envy or white as a sheet,
and wrinkles can show our age.

The look of despair, the open-eyed wonder,
the twinkle in the eyes,
the yawn that can't be stifled at all
no matter how one tries.

Jaw-dropping in surprise, a desperate look,
a haughty nose in the air;
a look of gloom, a look of doom,
starry-eyed and that curious stare.

We whistle a tune, grimace and snicker:
we scowl and also sneer.
If looks could kill, we show contempt,
disdain and a feeling that's clear!

One sticks out one's chin and takes a chance,
facing problems head on.
We can show a look of astonishment,
and also look pale and wan.

We purse our lips and shut eyes to small slights,
and are bleary-eyed after a wild night.
We've heard of startled looks when unusually dressed,
and getting a black eye in a fight.

One licks one's lips in anticipation,
and there's no masking that look of surprise;
and it's hard to conceal our disappointments
and happiness when winning a prize!

And, a "poker face" can conceal and deceive:
we interpret and play the game, too!
But, expressions sometimes are beyond our control,
like looking at a baby and coo!

ANTICIPATION

Some nerd in a garage is already at work,
ready to re-define our world:
like how to make water from the air,
or clothes that cannot be soiled!

Pressing a button will offer a cooked meal;
or an energy source very small.
Some kid will easily invade our privacy
with a lens that'll see through a wall!

My goodness, they're smart with fresh insights and skills:
nothing's beyond their grasp!
I won't be here to see it, but I'll watch from afar:
assuming that somebody's still here to gasp!

Simple Truth

I've been around the block, I'd say,
and have seen many things.
I've watched the folks at war and play:
a witness to slings and dings!

Everyone brings his bias and likes;
the exceptions are rarely seen.
I've come to terms with unanswered questions:
but I've learned about fat and lean!

If eating's your thing, or when hunger prompts you
to ask for that sandwich or plate,
your choice is important of cook or preparer:
for therein lies your culinary fate!

On the surface, it's amusing, but there's a nugget of truth.
(I've observed this time and again.)
Avoid Frail Fannie, whose meal portions are small;
choose, instead, chef Fat Hungry Ben!

Public Domain

I recently visited the Henry Lowenstein Art Museum,
one of our better known local attractions,
and was impressed with the personal connections
of the building's physical dependence
on its sponsors, donors and friends.

But, such dependence had its price.
For example; I entered through the Lily Kramer lobby
to a counter with a plaque indicating
that all chairs, desks and curtains
were the gifts of Ralph and Eleanore Kirby.
The large floral display was a gift of Dan Kirschner.

I stopped for a sip of water from
the Joshua and Sadie Goldman water fountain,
and proceeded to the Ralph and Murial Cassidy
gallery to see a show on loan from Joe and Jill Peters.
I rested for a moment on the Jenny Schwartz bench.

Next, I proceeded to the Edward and Alice Pushkin
Pavilion, picked up a brochure paid for by Hilda Love,
Feeling a bit hungry, I stopped at the Emily Kane
snack bar for a coffee and danish, beneath a mural
donated, as the plaque said, by Barney and Sue Bush.

Thus refreshed, I walked up the Bessie Greenwald stairway
to the second floor level and the Brian and Sylvia
Bobkin Gallery. Again being tired, I sat down on a bench
dedicated to Rose Williams, paid for by her garden club.

Needing a rest room, I entered the Steven and Linda Kessler
Men's Room, whose plaque informed me of their membership
since 1992.

The subsequent galleries were the Jesse and Brenda Stuart Room,
and the Carl and Sonia Tobin Young Artists gallery.
In each, there was provided a bench with its own donor name.

I finally stopped for a few minutes at the
Jack and Sarah Steiner souvenir and Gift Shop,
and left through the Paul and Stewart Garden exit,
through a gate donated by Benjamin and Joan Horowitz,
on a path of slates, each one of which bore
its donor's name, past a pool whose donor was
Donald and Emma Richter, in the middle of which was
an impressive bronze sea-horse, the gift of Bertha Dodd.

It was a busy day and I was relieved to return
to my apartment, aptly named the Nathan and Janet
Polsky Dwelling within the Zuckerman Towers Building.

Envy

I saw two birds cavorting and splashing
in a small fountain in a park.
It was so amusing and guaranteed
to lighten any mood that's dark!

They didn't mind my being there,
as if they were putting on a show.
They surely knew I was envious:
in such heat, how couldn't they know!

They didn't mind my stare and smile
(how I wished to share their pleasure!)
but, city life with its cement and bricks
doesn't offer such a grown-up treasure!

On a hot, humid day who wouldn't wish
to join those frolicking birds.
But, all I can do for now, at least,
is to describe my delight in words!

Political Realities

The lobbyists write the laws, it's said:
they offer bribes and cash.
Money is needed for campaigns,
which should be no news flash!

Our Congress should represent our will
(Representation is the democratic word!).
But, power rules, and the turnstiles work.
Or so I've read and heard!

The smartest brains and professional skills
are bought to squeeze and delude:
to create the sham that's our political life.
Or am I being rude?

The loudest drums assail our ears,
and create the dust we breathe,
with deceptive ploys and voting tricks,
which should make we victims seethe!

We fall for scams and Pied Piper tunes,
not knowing where our interests lie.
We are all victims and accept on cue
that proverbial pie in the sky!

Electing those who really speak for us,
is the only hope I see:
where special interests don't master us.
Until then we're never free!

Calendar Tid-Bits

When I was seven or eight, I'd look longingly
at the handles and straps
so high above my head, in the train or trolley,
beyond my midget-y reach:
mastered so easily by the "grown-ups".

Playing in an imaginary cave
beneath the dining-room table,
after a family meal or special occasion,
I remember being lost among the shins and legs
of uncles and aunts and cousins
noisily conversing above.
It was an adventure in a small person's world,
darkened by the over-hanging tablecloth.
It was a private sanctum where I hid and reigned.

When telling my age, it was always with
a grave emphasis on "...and a half!",
as if approaching grown-up status
could be hastened, or jostled
even just a little bit.

The short pants making way for the knickers, then long pants,
covering baby flesh with wool, and a belt!
I was on my way!

Playing "house" with sibling and cousins,
role-playing the "father",
and with story-telling "You must be..."
and "I must be...", chafing at time's harness,
impatiently waiting for our own truly adult turn.

The eager joy of being appointed blackboard
monitor by a friendly teacher responding
to my frantically waving upstretched arm,
practically screaming "Pick me! Pick me!".
It was such a special responsibility and honor
within our small classroom universe,
an award rewarded by inhalation of chalk dust!

And those colorful, skinny candles on birthday cakes,
awaiting my final, eager puff,
publicly pronouncing one step closer
to being "older",
adding another tree-ring, with nature's blessing,
accompanied by funny hats and colored balloons.

It was all part of the road stretching to now!

A Likely Story

The heart beat's steady, there's lack of pain:
all organs working fine;
all senses sharp, the vision's clear:
it's a wishful dream of mine.

No limp, no lump, no rash, no itch,
blood flow a normal pace;
no strain, no ache, no ungainly weight:
It's a hand with king and ace!

The back is straight, the muscles firm,
the brain is alert and clear.
There is no need for hearing aids,
and no virus hovers near!

The stomach accepts whatever it's given;
no wrinkle dares to show!
The lungs are strong, my memory's great,
my skin has a a wondrous glow!

Charley's horse and Arthur's ritus
are no friends I care to know
Ample hair is upon my head.
I'm immune to wind and snow!

So, please, won't someone wake me up
and applaud my imagination.
What's described above is fantasy land:
for we humans are a flawed creation!

Pulp Idol

Lone rider
sitting tall, erect in saddle,
from nowhere to nowhere.
Clean shaven, clear-gazed, impassive,
exuding calm, inner strength.

Timely arrival, as if ordained,
to solve town problem, dispute, inequity,
exact retribution, bring justice, right wrongs,
remove villain, troublemaker, tyrant, crooked officials,
uniting townfolk to stand firm, organized,
successfully removing evil.

Modest, no acclaim sought,
parrying aside townfolk's thanks,
rejecting gratitude or gifts,
turning away from inviting, enticing maidens,
moving on silently,
as when first appearing.

The western pulp magazine with its colorful cover,
overwhelming this wide-eyed young kid.
Cherished memory, vivid to this day!

Gratitude

My mother came here as a young, unschooled girl,
innocent, honest and alone.
An aunt took her in and she worked as all did,
coping in a motherless zone.

What a memory trove is a boyhood's past;
what little things come to mind,
that cling with a grip unmindful of time,
and bring smiles of a reminiscing kind.

She was a strong daily presence writ memorably large,
as a boy growing up years ago.
I speak not of cooking and cleaning and such,
but her nurture in helping me grow.

She was patient and protective with a mother's concern;
she hovered when I was hurting or ill.
She was warm and attentive and so proud of her son:
to this day I remember it still!

Little events come to mind, enmeshed in my brain:
bringing galoshes to school when it rained,
and her pride whenever I brought home a good mark,
or whatever achievement I attained.

Once, not completing a homework assignment,
and before classes were about to begin,
she came to school with paper, pen and ink
to avoid a scholarly sin.

When I entered the SoapBox Derby event,
where we built our racing cars to win,
she took me to the event by train,
seeing her son receive a prize pin!

I was not an easy young guest in our house:
it embarrasses me to say why.
I can only admire my mother's endurance and calm,
as for many years, my bed wasn't dry!

There are so many more images that time hasn't erased.
(Remembering is why I have misty eyes.)
She was self-less and provided a safe haven of care.
Her early loss can't help but bring sighs!

So, a belated "THANK YOU!" I offer to her,
my buddy and friend growing up.
Did she help shape and lovingly form what I am?
It's a resoundingly grateful "YUP!"

Curious

What would make a celery stalk,
or somebody get in a pickle?
Why does a smart man know his onions?
Why does a baby laugh when you tickle?

I'm not very wise, so help me with this:
What's the connection between a diamond and carrots?
Why do some green grapes have no pits?
And who gave the name "POLLY" to parrots?

What's the recipe to make a smart cookie?
Why is some girl called a "dish"?
And if a baby's so cute you could just eat it up,
isn't that a cannibal's wish?

Someone once told me to make hay when it shines:
Do I need a plaid shirt and blue jeans?
I asked a farmer what seed made a shrimp,
and he said I didn't know beans!

I always thought a well was a hole in the ground.
Are there three when I hear "Well! Well! Well"?
Is a cashew called that because it sneezes a lot?
Why do nuts have a shell?

Why is a bad car called a "lemon"?
How do you keep "one eye peeled"?
Why is a pretty girl "some tomato"?
How does one know when to yield?

Does shaking one's leg get you there any quicker?
Does "drink in the view" satisfy thirst?
Why does one want to shoot an innocent breeze?
Does excessive pride make you burst?

Do you give a fig if turned down for a date?
When in trouble why are you in a jam?
Also called a "fine kettle of fish!"
When is a sweet potato a yam?

Why does everyone call a lettuce a "head"?
And a-between-meal snack a munch?
Why is an important man called a "big cheese"?
Why is a suspicion a "hunch"?

So many questions, and so little time!
I've just begun to ask!
Life's a challenge, but I do want to know,
and peer behind our language mask!

Consumed

Cereal boxes get narrower, candy bars shrink;
the five-and-dimes are now dollar stores.
They'll sell you a row boat, if that's what you want:
but you'll have to pay extra for oars.

We're buffeted about with parking and fines;
bridge tolls are banking transactions.
Whatever you buy is a test of your calm:
all hint at worst coming attractions!

If you happen to have saving or other accounts
it's as if you must pay for the privilege.
With interest and taxes, penalties and fees:
we're victims of burn, slash and pillage!

Monetize is the word of our times:
increasing profits with stealth.
Businesses now use every angle and twist,
determined to reduce your wealth!

We're meek little sheep, sheared down to our skin,
losers in games out of control:
helpless consumers, milked like a cow,
victims hanging on to our soul.

We're squeezed until our nickels pop out,
we're innocents with no place to go,
Prices and costs go up as we speak:
it's impossible to save any dough!

Playtime

Where have all the rattles gone?
What's happened to old-fashioned toys?
We old-timers nostalgically remember:
they brought such childish joys!

Now I watch as diapered geeks
press buttons and pictures appear!
Those little devils will be smarter than me,
and making it abundantly clear!

Those computers, smart phones, I-Pads and such:
those are the toys of today.
Who knows with what *their* children will play
when they themselves become gray?

Devil's Garden

The growing trees and shrubs and grass,
all thrive with season's kiss:
they'll drink and sup from earth's home depths,
innocent with unknowing bliss!

The sun and rain and nature's touch
shroud a hidden past:
for beneath the roots and tendrils' growth,
lay scattered a woeful cast!

The blood and all that once was real,
now feed the thriving blooms.
The powdered ash and venom's fright
bespeak man's descent and dooms.

With memory sealed, the world moves on;
but never must we forget:
we harbor, still, the devil's sin,
and to deny is a loser's bet!

The soil of earth from mankind's start,
recites our deadly guilt:
whatever cause or hatred's birth,
death covers like a monstrous quilt!

Thus, whispering leaves mask ghostly moans
and breezes muffle sobs.
But, there is still no calm as pages turn:
we're still victims of hatred's mobs!

Revealed!

Peering through my aging's moss,
my younger years appear,
revealing scenes of family visits,
encounters you might wish to hear.

Each family, in turn, would visit and chat
comparing immigrants' notes,
like coping with life in this unfamiliar world:
the goal of steerage in boats.

Uncles and aunts, with yiddish-tinged talk,
joked and played cards for some fun:
where every pot of nickels and dimes,
would bring smiles from whoever had won;

While the socializing grown-ups shared gossip and such,
we small cousins would seriously play
our games of fantasy, "teacher" and "house",
as the hours darkened the day.

And now that those elders have long passed away,
I can reveal my secret at last.
For, if they had known at that time of my sin,
I'm sure they'd all be aghast!

We youngsters were allowed to nap on the bed
where the coats were casually strewn,
and I'm now embarrassed having to say
what I did, known only to the moon!

I was a "bed-wetter" then, and apologize now
to those departed kin of my youth,
who smelled that strange odor on their coats:
I'm unburdened that they now know the truth!

CHARISMA

The crowd roared its approval to see such a sight,
for, there I was standing over a lion so meek!
It stared at me with tears in its eyes:
certainly now no one could claim I was weak!

Picture a lion so humbled, and still,
pleading for mercy, a tear on its cheek!
Imagine my swelled ego and masterful core:
a beast at my feet, no bellow or squeak!

Handkerchiefs waved, for such a sight was unknown!
The awe was so rampant: could this be some dream?
The world stopped to marvel, and I knew then and there;
they'd have to admit I was not what I seem!

I wore a long cape with "NP" on its back.
I could fly and leap, lift weights by the ton!
Just then, my damn doorbell burst my balloon:
and with a loud crash ended my fun!

So, I placed my stuffed lion back on the shelf,
and, sadly, became my true timid self!

Valentine Poem

We're called a crowd if three or more;
sailors on ships are a crew.
A lot of fish is called a school
This poem says "I love you!"

A bunch of wolves is called a pack,
lots of bees a swarm.
A monkey group is called a tribe;
an army of ants can harm.

A family of lions is called a pride,
elephants travel in herds.
Many sheep are called a flock:
flock also applies to birds.

Geese enjoy their friendly gaggle,
a pod is a group of whales.
A colony is where the penguins live;
a bevy is a bunch of quails.

Kittens make a beautiful litter,
snakes coil in a lair.
A gang of partridge is a covey;
you and I are called a pair!

Witness

We met them on one of our European tours,
this woman and her younger boyfriend;
both friendly and talkative and fun to be with,
with no preview of our trip's end.

He was smiley and joking with no clue one could see,
of what we would witness soon:
for, slowly, his demeanor made it very plain
that he was becoming crazy like a loon!

The transformation before us was shocking to see,
from easy banter to scowling and curse.
We soon learned the truth which I share with all now:
he suffered from dementia and worse!

For he was a victim of a psychotic disorder,
requiring constant pills each day.
As long as he followed this drug-taking routine,
he appeared and acted normal, I'd say.

But his bottles of drugs were lost on this trip,
and his slow change was dangerous to watch.
He could be violent and yell and scary and wild,
below the insane scale by a notch!

We were so grateful to see the end of this tour
with our very lives intact.
But it impressed upon us the miracle of medicine,
··· the gift of normalcy. That's a fact!

Nasal Recall

Our sense of smell is a component of memory
that we associate with experiences past.
Whether conscious or not, it's a part of ourselves,
and, as long as we live, it will last.

The smell of mom's kitchen… or favorite dish,
the hay in the barn where we played.
The perfume of past love, incense in a house,
a repellent that we once sprayed.

A memorable garden of roses and mulch,
the pipe smoke that sweetened the air;
the marshmallow's fire, the spring's camphor balls,
the barber's tonic that flattened my hair.

There are so many memorable sniffs I recall,
but the single most meaningful to me,
is the art studio's oil paint and turpentine
which I inhaled with such ambition and glee.

I can still smell the talcum when my-babies were cleaned:
our nose is our memory's jog:
it returns us to moments buried and forgotten,
a peek through today's living fog.

Frontal Crudity

Sweatshirts and T-shirts are public billboards
displaying for the world to see:
a message, a slogan, a group or a thought.
It's a sharing and it's all for free!

Silk-screened in front or on back to be viewed,
is a word, a symbol or more.
Whether it's "PEACE' or "LOVE" in letters writ large,
or some image you cannot ignore.

But the funniest words in the smallest of type,
once decorated a young woman's chest,
saying "if you can read what's printed here
you're a pervert and a nosy pest!"

Read All About It!

What horrors await to be read today:
who murdered and who raped whom?
Who hit and run, who robbed a store?
Which scientist prophesied doom?

Which tyrant soldier overthrew another tyrant
to enrich himself instead:
to be the recipient of mineral riches
and protector of oil and well fed?

Wars still rage on, the corrupt among us get caught;
people-sheep vote to be sheared.
Democracy's way has been diverted and bought:
our future deserves to be feared!

The poor get poorer, the rich ones rejoice;
violence fills pages of print.
We read about poisoning land, sea and air:
optimism is barely a hint!

Who divorced whom, and how many victims were shot?
What natural disasters occurred?
Big companies buy smaller ones, stocks rise and fall.
I can see why the comic page is preferred!

Harvest

Little babies soon grow up,
and, in turn, they have their own.
And so, we humbly watch the crop,
from seeds that we have sown.

The magic of the flowering kin
could end with a blink or nod.
The scale of life and death depends
on blundering man or God!

Taking The Sun

Three turtles sit on a rock in a pool:
I cannot hear them speak.
They're utterly silent, thinking their thoughts;
I'd welcome even a squeak!

Are they related and have family ties?
Do they speak Turtle-ese we can't hear?
They quietly sit, unmindful of me,
head protruding without fear.

Are they huddled for social or gossipy exchange?
Do they realize the perfect picture they make?
If I snapped and entered that picture for a prize,
"BEST OF SHOW" is a piece of cake!

How they have sex is a mystery to me:
that shell is a hindrance, for sure!
That problem was solved a long time ago.
My nosiness doesn't detract from their allure!

Business Of Life

The path meanders (What a lovely word!):
clouds play with a sinking sun.
The air is still, there is no breeze;
dusk, and another day is done.

We turn the door sign around to "CLOSED",
and take one last look at the day.
Then, count our receipts and tally the losses:
thinking of tomorrow's dragons to slay.

Wild Ride

The entry-level hire can become the boss;
the rookie can become the Chief.
The ordinary looking kid with a smile,
may grow up to be a cop or a thief.

The old move on, next in line fill the gap:
it's an endless parade in time.
The escalator moves to niches and jobs:
from success to can you spare a dime!

It's not always the case of winning your way;
we're often swirling leaves in the tide:
helpless or lucky as fortune decrees,
high or swallowing pride.

The whim of the market, often no fault of our own,
can harden or shrivel our skin.
We're sometimes just commodities:
life's a raffle to lose or to win.

Square pegs in round holes, life's stumbles and puzzles,
hoping to land safe and secure.
Our ride's seldom smooth: we hang on for dear life.
It's a wonder how we can endure!

All Is Not Lost

We may lose our umbrella or our key,
inconveniences, to be sure.
But, loss surrounds us throughout our lives:
it's a miracle that we endure!

Our innocence goes as we grapple with life.
Lost opportunities occur all the time.
We lose control, our temper and sleep;
loss of ambition thwarts our climb.

There are so many fights for a lost cause,
and casualties of battles and war.
We lose our passion and our youth,
or the love that we adore.

We may lose our way, or lose our touch,
or even our place in line.
But, if we lose our cool when we lose our way,
our reputation will lose its shine.

Losing one's hearing, vision or hair,
may cause one to lose one's vanity
One shouldn't lose poise when losing a bet;
and when troubled, we shouldn't lose sanity!

Living's a game of coping with loss,
and sometimes we may lose the race.
But, as long as we don't lose our grip or our soul
we survive: like a lawyer losing a case!

Surprising Encounters

Sitting at a fast food counter,
wrapped in private thought,
the last thing I expected happened:
a surprise I never sought.

The woman seated next to me
turned to me and said
"You're bill's already paid by me!"
My face, I'm sure, turned red.

She smiled and told me to accept her gift.
I was frozen in my seat.
We talked awhile with small chit-chat.
I couldn't refuse her treat.

She then got up, saying she had to go.
My surprise had reached its peak.
But, without another word,
she kissed me on my cheek!

I told my wife of this encounter,
and that I didn't know what to do.
She said I made the whole thing up:
but I swore the story's true!

Something similar had happened before.
My wife and I went out to eat,
and a couple nearby paid our bill.
The waiter said it was their treat!

We never know what surprise awaits:
there are nice people who respond to whim.
I'm always ready to make them happy,
when their impulse overflows their brim!

But, was it pity for the way I dressed,
or was it my sorrowful face?
Because, if this were so, for sure:
I'd try to refuse with grace!

Attuned

Purple is a lovely color,
soothing and restful, too,
not contentious or speed inclined,
my friend with green and blue.

Such colors clearly set a tone,
so far from frenzied red,
and bring a tranquil inner peace.
I'm sure you've heard it said.

My colors bring reprise and calm
(we respond in our own way).
They shield and help to shut out din:
medication for my day.

But sometimes I hear a whimpering sound,
as if by a neglected fellow;
and I contritely admit my sometime affection
for an uplifting, companionable yellow.

Now, compassion compels me not to offend,
so I'll give the devil his due.
I'll honestly admit my moments of highs,
and pay homage to the reddish hue, too!

A Grallo's Tlo

(A poetic communication from an outer planet)

The yummies scatter pratts and mools
by the light of salavas.
But aflot.habott and shoomy shar
dance with the sharazaz.

The raltos skit along the waits
to see what proxy does,
as holdican berates the zold
and sings a mellow fluz.

Now, it happened that farzon soofed
to show his lotty's hak;
but gluny's hess befoled the way
annoying coro's lomak.

And so it went, the ashpic's hiss,
blakens ashowaw lup;
Hitto kept pokaly's zat,
and noone gave a frup!

Where I Draw The Line!

Let me draw your attention to something quite odd:
a word used in so many ways.
If you draw a blank when I make this assertion,
let's discuss this multi-use maze.

We draw a distinction between certain things;
we draw a conclusion, as well.
When we think we're not wanted we withdraw.
When drawing a winning number, it's swell!

Sometimes we are overdrawn at the bank,
and we're suddenly filled with dread.
We'd like to have someone to draw and quarter,
but, we draw a deep breath, instead.

In battle, we're likely to draw enemy fire.
As an artist, we would just like to draw.
In summer, we're likely to draw mosquitoes and flies;
cowboys saying "DRAW!", we abhor.

We're sometimes inconvenienced by a draw-bridge;
we draw water from a well.
We draw from our experience;
we draw strength, from where I can't tell.

There are some from whom we draw inspiration,
I know you must agree.
We look drawn and tired as we age:
It's no fun, believe you me!

The Pendulum's Arc

So, where was I before the wind
disheveled my hair
and blew my poem's outline on to the ground
under the bench.

There are so many thoughts clinging to the page,
looking up at me with dust-filled eyes
asking for a sympathetic lift and hug.
Which, of course, I willingly do.

So much to say, to ponder, to share,
to sift through memory's screen
until the grains of value settle
into the final fill of cherished recall.

I still hear the sounds of my daughters'
playful laughter and rapt attention;
listening to my made-up improvised pre-bed tales,
of Indian folks and adventures;
of their Halloween cat dress with long stuffed tails,
devised lovingly by their mother cat Janet,
with eyebrow and penciled chin and cheek whiskers,
seeking to impress and extract, hopefully,
another treat or two.

The slowly emerging young ladies with diverging path
of interests, traits, habits, personalities,
each seeking definition, self-expression, independence:
then, college, marriage, departures, new families:
enabling us to become loving spectators
of their own unique orbits and cycles.

It's a journey, told and retold countless times.
Janet and I have become the autumn and winter,
cheering on the spring and summer
of our children morphing, inexorably,
as adults toward senior-hood themselves.
We watch, embrace—no, accept—the chill of inevitability.

What is the fifth season beyond winter?

TOGETHERNESS

Some words and phrases are common to us:
they've acquired a long life through use.
We respect them as our useful friends,
even if they suffer abuse.

Custom has combined them as conjugal siblings:
they've become rooted in habit and thought.
Repetition through usage helps us to know
and it's really not all for naught.

It tickles my fancy as I chew on this,
and accept it as fair and square,
these often used and conjoined mates,
such as a table and chair.

Bits and pieces, trick or treat,
lavish praise, hard as nails;
a grueling effort and flushed with success:
Now choose if heads or tails.

It's only a figment of imagination;
lost in thought and a winning smile;
shake like a leaf and bone of contention,
as sad as a miser's pile.

At a loss for words and easy virtue,
first and foremost and top drawer;
buck the trend and ebb and flow,
no one likes blood and gore.

Take a deep breath, breathe a sigh of relief,
Certainly not, by a long shot;
entertain an idea, a passing fancy.
blunt advice, thanks a lot!

In a stupor and in the long run,
dragging kicking and screaming;
it was a tall tale and beyond belief:
features that are not redeeming.

Most assuredly and duly noted,
a paltry sum, perish the thought;
with telling effect and spur of the moment,
a cold's very easily caught.

Give a blank look and paper shuffler,
seeing eye to eye;
unmitigated gall, spewing venom,
nobody likes a wise guy!

An off-hand remark, and money talks:
rue the day and it took its toll,
music to my ears and that so and so,
we won't touch with a six foot pole.

Rub the wrong way and up in the air,
unexpectedly thrown for a loop;
dyed in the wool and living it up,
free after flying the coop!

Blissfully ignorant, wax and wane,
having a quizzical look;
flight of fancy, ball and chain,
the sound of a babbling brook.

In the nick of time, in a fog and a daze;
a comic cracking a joke;
shoes and socks, comb and-brush,
no one likes a slow poke.

Hale and hearty, strong and able,
try to take it in stride;
rack and ruin, rain cats and dogs,
best wishes to groom and bride.

A leap of faith, all is pitch black,
a face that's pale and wan;
black and blue, odds and ends,
gosh, I could go on and on!

Remembering

The little boy sits on a cafeteria stool
opposite a grown suited man
waiting patiently, each nursing
a hot-watered, lemoned cup,
waiting for the appearance
of the child's second floor neighbor,
who, as everyone knew,
habitually frequented the place
for his after-work snack
of coffee and pie.

As the hour was slowly passing,
the child fretted and wished
he was playing his interrupted games
of ball and marbles,
or creating his own sailing vessel
of folded paper and stick mast
with its curved paper sail,
floating along the puddling curbside water,
the residue of a watering truck
flushing the street.

But, his mother volunteered his services
as a favor to her friendly neighbor's needs.

Suddenly, he straightened up
and, excitingly, said "There he is!"
pointing to a short-bodied fellow
in an overlarge jacket just entering.

Upon which the table companion jumped to his feet,
pulled out a folded paper,
and, briskly, walked over to the identified man
and handed it to him, to his utter surprise and consternation.
It was a subpoena, properly served,
for a court appearance in a suit for child support.

The child's duty done, he was thanked,
given a nickel, and taken home, to his mother's satisfaction,
at being a sympathetic, helpful neighbor.

I was that little boy.

That Old Philco And Emerson

Well before television. Before cell phones.
Before whatever satisfies our
entertainment needs today,
there was that wonderful magic box
in our living room somehow sheltering
adventure, advice, concerts,
story telling continuing every week,
eagerly awaited.

Companion on a sick day: pre-bedtime family hearth,
opening up cerebral imagery
to accompany the voices and sounds
entering our spellbound, eager ears.

Oh, those weekly heroes, those villains,
cowboys, justice-bringers, unseen friends,
jokesters: all giving pleasure, escape,
company, knowledge and exposure
to the world of culture and fun!

Without accompanying sight,
the mind filled in the gaps,
visualizing the heard, but, unseen!
Imagination thrived.
Radio made possible the flowering of
participatory imagination!

It was so pre-microwave!

Overdose

Once, in grade school, our teacher
took our class to a nearby
children's science museum
to experience the exhibited
and hands-on displays.

To this day, I cannot eat a banana
without wincing!

For, at that elementary school's visit,
there was an exhibit stressing
the differing odors of nature's products,
by pressing the appropriate button.
I pressed too long and inhaled
an overlarge dose of banana!
Yes, overdose!

The smell still lingers as I write.
If such overdosing were illegal then,
I would just now be eligible for parole!

Pictorial

I can barely see the arcing bridge
through the hazy fog.
The bay is silent and vacant.

The scene is impressive
for its lonely visual pleasure,
wedding nature and intrusive man.

On a clear day, the cars
are like marching ants
following an elevated trodden path
to forage or fight.

The gulls and their distant cousins
sit atop a row of vacant poles,
residue of some extended pier,
once providing water-sport pleasure
in some distant past.

To our ears there is silence,
no neighborly exchanged gossip,
each squatter lost in avian thought:
innocent contributors to
cell phone art.

Adrift

Muse, oh Muse, I sorely need your help!
I sit and try to grasp that slippery evasive concept,
playing with my eagerness to capture my prize.

My mind is blank with fatigue and impatience;
but the well is dry, and I note
a sassy thumb to the tip of your nose.

Have I run through the gamut of ideas,
insights and observations
once guiding and flowering my path?

I'm tired. I'll wait.
Tomorrow, my ink will flow again.

Pretty please!

Just Wondering

A doctor's waiting room
is where you patiently wait
to hear your name called.

Is that why you are called a patient?

Why is it called a "practice"?
When does the doctor become a professional
and is through "practicing"?

Does a missed appointment
constitute a disappointment?

Why in the world is a cranky person
called a "pill"?
And, certainly, not to have to take
even once a day!

Good weather or bad, it's not surprising
to. see a stethoscope scarf
around a doctor's neck.

A Hopeless Wish

My daughters, my grandchildren, their spouses,
progeny yet to be,
looking serious with bouts of sadness
and happiness: the gamut of life's offerings,
more lines in faces,
slower pacing, graying heads.

The great-grandchildren with their own
children and great-grandchildren,
nibbling, in turn, at their own unfolding,
unwinding universe, nursing new mysteries
with accompanying griefs and tears,
but also with laughter buttressing
against the solemn realities within time's domain:
surrounded by new souls,
one of whom might be named Nathan.

My unphysical eyes, a wanderer within the winds,
observe, in silent witness, jealously, regretfully.
so longing to re-appear and be, once more,
a player-participant in what would never be.

The story continues beyond the familiar chapters
of my once-living presence,
when flesh and love thrived:
and am saddened by the reluctant distance,
the historical sweeps beyond my own
physical moment, when alive.

I will be that face in the frame
on a great-grand-child's wall:
a reminiscence, an ancestor.

My wife, a fellow vintaged traveler,
will entwine her fingers in mine, and, together,
in silence, will thankfully peek and
linger for just awhile longer.

Menders

The human body has been divided
into convenient pieces for inspection and repair.

There is a specialist for ears, liver, eyes,
nose, bladder, teeth, knee, hip, heart, feet,
toes, bones, skin, intestines, brain, nerves,
lungs, hair, kidneys, blood, etc.
Not to mention allergies, illness, disease.

The doctor is a mechanic
where we go to have our corroded
and broken parts salvaged or replaced.
We go to his garage to have our tires rotated,
get a new fan belt or fuel pump,
or just an oil change.
But our odometer is what it is.

And, if we're lucky, and have driven carefully,
there may yet be some value
in the older, vintage models.

Helpful ID

Those letters after a person's name
designating a professional role
such as MD, PH.D, CPA,
or degrees earned or honors achieved,
suggests an interesting way of providing
immediate identification or recognition
of anybody's interests, status, social role
or self-description.

Such letter combinations may be self-assigned
or bestowed by general consent.

For example:

HW	House wife	CG	Care giver
BW	Bread Winner	HO	Home Owner
PW	Postal Worker	PP	Patient Parent
OH	Over the Hill	SAL	Swindler-at-Large
LOD	Living Off Daddy	LOO	Living Off Others
OP	One Percenter	SD	Sanctimoniously Divine
ST	Selfish Taker	HGK	Heavenly Gate-Keeper
LP	Lord's Pipeline	CC	Chronic Complainer
PP	Professional Politician	HM	Honest Merchant
WDD	Whoop-Dee-Doer	MHBS	Master of Hold, Buy, Sell
SG	Stock Gambler	IT	Independent Thinker
AH	Always Hungry	HB	Home Body
WE	Wandering Eye	SAC	Selfish As They Come
CA	Conceited-Ass	DH	Domestic Helper

A Narcissist's Poem

Around us there are certain folks,
and I wish them out of sight!
They hover with their ego's ice:
and this is the poem they'd write!

Me-Me, Me-Me, Me-Me, <u>Me</u>!
Me-Me, Me-Me, <u>Me</u>!
Me-Me, Me-Me, Me-Me, <u>Me</u>!
Me-Me, Me-Me, <u>Me</u>!

I'm vaguely aware you're somewhere there
(please don't block my sun!)
You're the holes and I'm the cheese:
I hope you get the pun!

MIMI is such a pretty name:
it's a wonderful name for me.
Saplings are almost everywhere,
but I'm the stately tree!

God was lavish in his gifts;
I'm his perfect work!
Superior, smart with a wit that's quick
and a brain where angels lurk.

The rest of you just take up space,
and allow my haughty struts.
I'm my own sweet lover, with cause enough:
a pedigree versus mutts!

Nature's Payback

I'll get you yet if you push too far.
I'll cut you down to size.
You'll tease and test just once too often,
and you'll deserve your booby prize!

You're trying to take over the neighborhood,
a big shot and smarty-pants;
well, I've got a few surprises for you,
while you preen and prance!

I've been around a good long time,
before you were just a cell.
I've watched some folks create their heaven,
and some their devil's hell.

I provided elements and tools,
and saw what you could do.
Your brains just grew in marvelous ways,
but your wisdom lacked a clue!

It's squeeze and grab with selfish greed,
with no thought of those who follow.
You've drilled and mined and burned and slashed,
leaving mayhem in which to wallow!

So reap and feel the brunt you'll bear
of flood and storm and drought;
of chill and wind and parch and dry
and worse, there is no doubt!

You've ruined the seas and lives therein;
you've contaminated waters:
cancers, plagues and floods and storms
will hurt your sons and daughters.

You've made your home an angry place,
and to yourselves no less kind:
I may not have to do a thing:
your end, yourselves, will find!

Hollywood Preview

They were such a handsome pair,
the last to join our tour.
They both, we learned, were Hollywood types,
an obvious case of amour!

He was an agent of stars and such,
she was an opera singer.
He said this trip was a pre-nuptial gift,
before putting a ring on her finger.

Oh, how he laughed and loved to talk,
he wasn't shy at all.
He'd mingle and offer free Polaroid shots:
there was never a social wall!

So, off we'd go seeing sights by bus,
stopping for each overnight stay;
but that pretty girl always left something behind,
to the fellow's increasing dismay!

He'd have to find ways to re-trace the tour's steps,
and retrieve the bracelet or shoe.
Even her mink coat was left in a closet,
and we could witness a bubbling brew!

In addition, our required very early departures
started to turn his face livid.
His habit, we guessed, of rising at noon
made his obvious. annoyance vivid!

We watched as his friendliness and poise
turned glum as he glared at his friend.
Seeing her scatterbrain mind in the sky,
without sleep it was a bad blend!

By the time the tour ended, we could see this nice guy
slowly turn into a wreck of a man,
re-thinking his options and Hollywood life:
we guessed that he might change his plan!

ADIEU!

I really saw a frog today
(I hadn't seen one in years).
It was such a pleasure, for I'd heard they'd gone,
and I truly missed the dears.

It was a sodden gray and barely moved;
it seemed so forlorn and weary.
It rested alone beneath the bench in shade:
its sudden sight was eerie!

I love these little rascals so,
whose loss demeans us all.
I remember well their sight and sounds,
their rumbling, throaty call.

One by one our neighbors go
that thrived and added flavor,
victims of befouling, heedless greed,
depriving us of beauty to savor.

Their loss anticipates our very own,
"pristine" and "lush" just words.
For the moment's gain, we slowly die,
and join earth's fish and birds!

So, my little napping, dying frog,
sadly losing home and friends:
let's commiserate as brethren do,
and contemplate our respective ends!

Song Of The Vernacular

Tra-la-la and raz-ma-taz,
hunky-dory, wink and blink;
with an oo-la-la and a la-de-da,
my armor has a kink.

Willy-nilly and a hippity-hop,
everything's okey-dokey;
so holy moley and golly-gee,
how did I end up in the pokey!

Life is a lu-lu, never ho-hum;
it's a free-fall early from birth.
You can't sneak a peek and say "oh-my-gosh!"
nor choose between tears and mirth

So let's not poo-poo the future's "Oh-Oh"
or life's minor pish-posh.
Life giveth and taketh on this merry-go-round ride
and you'll miss friends with whom you could josh!

It's rah-rah for me and fiddle-faddle for you
as we crave any itsy-bitsy success;
there's always the chance for the heave-ho by Fate,
and we're left to clean up the mess!

Don't say gee-wiz or perish the thought,
palsy-walsy relations are few.
We live with the effects of life's little boo-boos:
there's no choice from the time we say "goo!"

So with a rinky-dink effort or shilly-shally wish,
lo and behold, you'll soon find out:
only fervor and patience despite all the pummeling
are the winners of a 30-round bout!

Dark Matter

Old age is a bummer, I now sadly admit:
my muscles aren't in prize form.
My breathing is labored and cold is no friend.
I've wandered far from the norm.

I've been through a war as a young sturdy fellow.
I've run miles with nary a pause.
I could chin myself up to thirty, at least,
and went to bed late just because.

I could go on and recite all that I've done
to prove that I was godly endowed:
so bright and so fast, you wouldn't believe.
I made my mother proud!

But, slowly and surely time takes its toll;
and as I look at the guys at the gym,
my old memories soothe, but jealousy darkens,
and I pine for my lost youth and vim.

I understand cycles of life and of death:
I don't expect to he an exception.
But wouldn't it be nice to lift two hundred pounds
before arriving at St. Peter's reception?

Be Gone!

There is this tale of Noah's ark,
that saved our threatened creatures.
But, I'm sorry that his welcome included
species with annoying features!

If he had sense and thought it through,
we'd enjoy life more today:
with no mosquitoes, ticks or lice,
and no need for traps or spray!

Who needs those ants and bugs and mites;
and what good are all those roaches,
or those pesky bedbug devils.
which we find so atrocious!

Our world's beset because of him,
with flying, crawling things,
that bite and suck and spoil our lives,
whether we be serfs or kings!

But, having made that fateful choice
to admit on that safety's ride
those destroyers of our calm and peace,
in defense, we kill where they hide!

Out come our spray cans, screens and traps,
flypaper with its glue,
poisoned powders, tablets, gas:
to defend and just say "SHOO!".

Memorable Moment

The lake was wide and the surface still,
except for slight rippling of wavelets
against the sandy shore.

The distant hills hovered around a colony
of barely distinct homes, miniature and mute.

A lovely white sail slowly crossed the lakescape vision,
to form the perfect touristy card.

The leisurely clouds captured the pictorial mood,
with shades of canopy purpley puffs
shielding an approaching darkening bluish dusk.

The serenity was magical, wrapped around silence,
except for a neighbor's occasional barking dog,
but not loud enough to disturb the scene and the moment.

A deep breath, a cerebral snapshot, an image recorded,
destined to replay itself countless times
to repudiate time's passage and tensions.

Some memories are like that.

Good Morning

Mirror, mirror on the bathroom wall,
who the hell is this face I see?
Hair unkempt, watery eyes with bags:
it can't possibly be the daytime me!

I see him whenever my day begins,
before I wash and comb and shave.
He frightens me and makes me shudder
at this character from some primitive cave.

This is not the face in my graduation book:
but, as my eyes adjust, and I know I'm he,
I accept what's there and get to work,
until ready for the world to see.

Collective Loss

His feet were large, he stooped a bit,
his walk was always slow.
He was tall and quiet and modestly dressed;
his voice was calm and low.

He was bright and smart, we all thought;
his grades were unusually high.
We whispered that he would go very far:
this fellow graduate, so shy.

We knew he'd make his mark in life.
(A little envy played its role!).
We agreed we'd later hear of him;
his brilliance would achieve his goal.

The years passed by, and then the war:
our studies had to cease,
as we were called to serve and fight,
and, hopefully, resume with peace.

We did our part, we fought and won:
but, there were some bitter dues.
We picked up threads of life we'd led,
and shared our trials and views.

But, to our sorrow and dismay,
we learned in voices hushed:
that brilliant scholar with so much promise
was killed, and his flower crushed!

Short Story

The jar of chocolate-covered raisins
sits silently, enticingly, coyly awaiting
its moment of sweetened solace
to the TV obsessed.
Me.

The pop corn, potato chips, pistachios:
all stand ready, bagged, boxed, handy,
primed for the searching fingers
and eager mouth.
Mine.

Challenge

A single sock stares up at me,
with a wrinkled laugh:
a mystery, a challenge, a mocking dare,
like a cow's little lost calf.

It becomes a test of Sherlockian skill,
a half-truth, a stunted whole.
It's make me so very humble and helpless;
Fate's victim, yet too proud to cajole.

The sock is thrown into the mystery drawer,
joining the key-less locks:
a useless trifle, an abandoned half-truth,
to join its fellow bachelor socks.

Basic Training

I had a dream the other night
which took me back in time:
I was a soldier boy again
and phone calls were a dime.

It was the big one we had to fight
to destroy that monster man,
who was destroying peace and threatened us,
and we had to thwart his plan.

In I went, an innocent kid
in my strange new army home;
it was an interesting time, I can recollect,
so, I thought I'd write this poem.

They struggled hard to change our ways,
from easy, undisciplined boys:
they cut our hair and taught us to obey,
and gave us military toys.

But what I recall the very most,
is the lingo we learned to share.
To a civilian's ears this will sound strange,
but this was our life laid bare.

The gold-brick strived to avoid all chores,
the sad sack was not up to par;
basic training made us get on the ball,
and salute to a gold bar.

You couldn't be out of uniform;
your foot locker was your home,
together with your barracks bag,
and I didn't sleep on foam.

Everything's done by the numbers
from reveille to lights out!
Roll call came before mess hall,
and your drill sargent was some lout.

You wore your dog tags all the time,
the food we ate was chow.
KP would be your punishment
ten push-ups sweated brow.

Rise and shine was morning's song;
hubba-hubba meant hurry up!
From time to time they'd let you rest,
we were each a helpless pup!

Latrine duty was a needed chore:
spotless was the word:
grungy work for some lucky soul
(it helped build character, I heard!).

Some took advantage and pulled rank,
some sucked up to get ahead.
Mail call was awaited eagerly,
and hit the sack meant bed!

Continued

our training tried to mold and shape
us into a fighting force:
from fall in—fall out—forward march,
at ease and about face, of course.

Hup-hup-hip-haw
was marching's vocal beat.
We also sang with raucus voice:
it was melody's help for feet.

"I've been working on the railroad
all the live long day…"
and "Someone's in the kitchen with Dinah!"
helped miles just melt away.

Left—two-three-four,
we marched until we heard "Halt!";
then "About face!" and then "Dismissed!":
we were slowly earning salt!

Of course, there's always more to share,
'til memory jogs no more.
But that young fellow, now so gray,
will not forget that war!

The Last Word

Our earthly garden lies bewildered and shorn
of bountiful gifts,
rejected and scorned
for selfish and suicidal nows.

Our Maker's glance and glare
at our defiling gift-spurning
and ungrateful contempt
for our provided home
will cause regret with no redress
to our collective shame and end.

Keeping Informed

I can hardly wait to sit and to read
of the events of the previous day,
to learn of the murders and floods and the crimes,
and to hear what the crooks have to say.

I'm a junkie for news like an addict with drugs
who must have his daily fix:
like who killed whom or bridges that fall
or a con man up to his tricks.

It's a carnival of characters that daily pass by:
the good and the terrible types:
the inventors, creators and entertainers, of course,
and some who just make you say "Yipes!".

The mayhem and struggles that envelop our lives,
the tragedies, discoveries and games:
who married, divorced and those caught in the act,
involving some well-known names.

I cringe at atrocities and genocide reports,
and victims of hunger and drought;
the tyrants and all those Presidents For Life!
Is this what our world is about?

As if natural disasters are not enough for our news,
or disease and poverty's scourge:
there's corruption and politicians who don't represent,
and the world's population surge.

But there's also diversions to brighten the day
and to help counter what's dismal and sad.
There's fashion and comics and what's going on,
and reports of the latest fad.

But what brightens my mood after shootings and rapes
is reading of the good ones among us,
the quiet, hardworking and honest folks,
who perform and contribute without fuss!

Renewal

When spring rouses like a hatchling's cracking egg,
I breath deeply the fragrant freshness of aborning life.

I sit and intake freshly minted air
with gulps like an ascending diver breaking water.

It's heady, intoxicating, dizzying, like remembered
pasts, but with renewed excitement
for living's new possibilities.

Gone is the layer of degraded, lifeless, sodden remnants
of leaves' prior glory, seasonally departed,
and the sheltered secret of a snowy-white quilt,
scenic or tire-tracked, now slowly dissolving,
its scripted performance completed
in the annual quartet of seasons.

Soon, the winged and legged creatures
will respond to the warming ambiance
and make laboring appearances, re-occupying
familiar air and turf: for it's renewal time.

Like past season's acorns, quietly alive
with wombed patience, and skies the doorway
to a heaven with billowing accent puffs,
restless, growing things thrive like energized puppets
in Nature's invisible dexterous hands.

For the moment, I stop my time's pace and simply am,
joining the rejuvenation.

Choices

The winner's circle is indeed quite small,
for few fellows have made it to the top.
Our presidents reflect our changing times,
and range from the great and the flop.

Our national needs and changing moods
call forth the proper one to lead;
we've been lucky with many of the choices made,
but sad with the unsavory deed.

It's hard to find wisdom in those we elect
who can help steer our ship of state
through shoals and impediments here and abroad,
so only a rare few can be called great.

Mt. Rushmore, of course, still honors just four
to remind us of examples we've found.
We get what we deserve and deserve what we get,
as we respond to our future's sound.

Hat Chat

The tops of our heads have stories to tell,
for it just takes a glance and we know:
for what's worn is a hint of a trade or a clue
of status, both high and the low.

Each cover on top, be it scarf or tiara,
helps us define taste and rank.
We don't have to guess or wonder aloud,
for the hat will fill in the blank.

It could be tradition, protection or style,
religion, respect or group norm;
or status or warmth or fashions to impress,
or desire to shock or conform.

The blue hat of the cop and sailors white caps,
the helmet, wool weave or beret,
fedora, chef hat, the fez and straw hat,
the stetson and skull cap to pray.

The baseball cap visor facing front or back;
the panama, bonnet or turban;
the mortar board of the graduate, pointed hat of the witch,
we all know, whether rural or urban.

The Cardinal's red cap, the derby so round,
the monk's cowl and royalty's crown;
the fisherman's felt hat with its hooks and its lures,
the bride with her veil and her gown.

The eskimo's hood and the Russian's fur lid,
the Pontiff's elaborate mitre;
the hasidic's traditional fur-trimmed cover,
the feathered Indian's decor is lighter.

And let's not forget the state trooper's flat brim,
or the top hat for a special event.
Sometimes we can hear the sounds of the less formal,
described as the hatless lament.

Balance

It's such a joy to be wrapped
in a blanket of private silence,
so solitude can water the dormant seeds
of a poem or any artistic activity.

The trick with such self-absorption
is maintaining a realistic, harmonious
balance with marital
or other social relationships,
beyond one's self.

Such deliberate withdrawal
demands a social price,
whatever the resulting product
or simple recharge.

Dark Thoughts

A dreadful thought's been bothering me,
that I would like to share.
What if this world should disappear?
It fills me with despair.

What a shame to lose all life,
all culture, self and kin;
all our human skill and brains,
disappearing in a nameless bin.

This nightmare thought could come to pass
because our gifts we spurn;
or erasing protective atmosphere,
when all life may succumb and burn.

It's also not remote to think
that we ourselves, of course,
will cause demise or weakened end
by uncivil or dogmatic force.

Or rampaging nature may decide our fate
with movement of earth or tide.
If come to pass, I shudder to think,
there'll be no place to hide.

Please forgive this speculative fright
that so disturbs my peace.
But if any of this should actually be,
all poetry would cease.

Persuasion

What would television be like
without somebody urging us to be
a timely and smart consumer!

We are implored to respond
by calling the number on the screen:
Call within the next ten minutes
for free samples, an astonishing
low price, no money dawn, free delivery,
unimaginable happiness and health,
unlimited erections (when the moment is right!),
and be the envy of your neighbors!

And if, for any reason, you are not satisfied,
return for a full refund!
There are low monthly payments;
and no payment required for two years!
If you order now, you'll be glad you did!
It's new and improved, a real breakthrough
in technology, even a life-altering experience,
and any color of your choice!
Not available in stores! Why settle for less!

But wait! There's more!
If you call now, we'll cut the price in half,
and, we will double the offer!
Two for the price of one! Don't delay! Hurry!
Only limited quantities available!
And the first fifteen callers will receive a special gift!

It's yellow pages in a new medium!

Shower

A bridal shower is to fill a bower
of practical gifts for a new life.
A list is suggested or guests try to guess
at the needs of the husband and wife.

The joy is the giving, and the receiving, as well,
and to celebrate the event that's ahead.
It's a form of good wishes in practical ways,
for those who are about to be wed.

I can accept this tradition, if it be so,
but the name "shower" has mystified me.
Is it for a light rain or a soapy rinse,
or watering for flowers to be.

I think it's a send-off to a new life for two:
a champagne bottle blessing a new ship,
embarking upon the matrimonial sea.
Please forgive this metaphorical quip.

Sales Pitch

Give me your money, savings and all,
trust me to care for it well.
My face is quite honest, as you readily see;
I'm your friend for only a slight fee.

I have the connections, the knowledge and smarts.
I assure you your money is safe.
I consult the heavens, Barron's and Forbes.
I gave money to save a waif.

The market's my game, my record's impressive.
I've brought wealth to many in town.
I know when to buy and I know when to sell.
The broker you now have is a clown!

Don't look at my gold cuff links or alligator shoes.
Don't look outside at my car.
My monogrammed shirt is what you can have, too.
Meeting me is your lucky star.

Mutual funds, oil pipelines and drilling at sea,
derivatives, start-ups and such:
invest in Africa, New Zealand and Japan
and you'll appreciate my knowledgeable touch.

Real estate is tempting, my sources all say,
so, invest now and have peace of mind.
I'll double your money', just sign this form here.
You'11 see I'm one of a kind.

Mate Search

Hop, skip, jump and pitter-patter,
don't ask me wherefores and why's.
We live and breathe in dribs and drabs,
at destiny's beck and sighs.

We slip and slide which is all well and good,
awaiting that wink and a nod.
Life's bric-a-brac offers mix and match,
So we may pick and choose, by God.

We win some, lose some, with trick or treat,
with available vigor and vim;
it's slow and steady, or fast and loose:
lickety-split and to the brim.

The nuts and bolts mix hope and despair:
when happy, it's hunky-dory.
But mish-mosh and pish-posh, like it or not,
a wrong choice is a colonial's Tory.

So, we wander and search, and respond if we can,
until a fit is achieved;
a blending of sorts, an ease and response;
Fate's purpose can then be believed.

Image

The reflecting glass was once my friend,
augmenting youth-fresh eyes,
but now looks at me with clucking tongue,
and filled with shameless lies.

I look in vain in hopes to find
that once young brand new me.
Instead, the silver mirror jeers
and pokes fun at what I see.
The silent circling of clocks' hands,
and with calendar pages torn,
and the parade of seasons past and gone,
I sense a welcome outworn.

I miss a face unlined, unpuffed,
unbagged and head-filled hair.
The roller coaster ride slows down;
when gone, I hope you care.

Delicious Memories

Oh, the taste of foods that come to mind
when thinking of things to eat:
our tongue's favorite friends soothe palette and taste,
and will always be welcome to greet.

Some dishes and treats take us back to our youth
reminding us of other places and time,
when momma served her yummy broiled chicken,
and hot dogs were only a dime.

And who can forget her hot chicken soup
and chopped liver and latkes to savor;
certainly not me when my eyes glaze at the thought
of holiday dishes with flavor.

My wife, when she cooked, tried to pick up the slack,
and eating again brought me pleasure:
the thanksgiving turkey, those chops and the roasts,
all contribute to my memory's treasure.

The corned beef and pastrami, I no longer can eat:
the half-sour pickles I adored,
are joys of the past and I can only whimper and fret.
Now so many foods leave me bored.

The tastes are like cardboard and seldom can match
what I now recall with such joy.
Who wants to fill up with foods made in haste,
pre-prepared or served cold…and with soy!

HA-HA-HA

What gear in our creature machine
produces a giggle,
and such other sounds of laughter
unique to us alone?

Is it, indeed, a "funny bone"?

A Bright Idea!

One day, there may be a way
for "downloading" a brain's contents:
its accumulated stored knowledge,
experience and memories,
which would otherwise be lost forever,
upon the death of the brain's owner.

Free To Fail

The game is over when winners' bounty
collects all cards and marbles,
and offers most others
dregs and dross:
and only enticing hope!

An Uncomfortable Truth

Our brains and living systems
are but supporting factories
to foster specie survival and continuity;
absorbing sustenance
to sustain this priority,
until advancing age intrudes
and offers no secondary
natural purpose for existence.

Bottled Poetry:
What A Copywriter Might Write!

A fresh and lively wine to drink,
with a young and vigorous taste,
makes for easy drinkability
and cannot result from haste.

With up-front aroma and hint of oak
and subtle spices, too,
with soft sweet tannins and mineral notes,
the taste is bound to woo.

You'll love the vintage and character
and nose of deep cherry fruit,
the structure and personality:
only low brows don't give a hoot!

Soft and creamy on the palate,
yet favoring plum and berry,
the round and flavorful richness and taste
persuades a drinker be merry.

Overflowing with inviting sniffs,
and an utterly delightful sip,
wines encourage sociability,
thirst-quenched in Bacchus's grip.

So, subtlety of nose and accompanied taste,
the smoky fruits and flavor,
like peach and orange and apricot
make wines a drink to savor.

You're Wasting Your Time

For crying out loud and well, well, well,
gee whiskers and my, oh, my;
oh, brother and a whatchamacallit,
whiz-bang and a good college try!

Ye God's and all the little fishes, as well;
by golly and now, now, now;
jimmy cricket, hot dog, you betcha, wink, wink
hee-haw I cannot allow!

By heck and c'mon and check-mate, too,
come again and get outa here!
It's yak, yak, yak and yadda, yadda, yadda,
complain and you can kiss my rear!

You think you're a shoo-in to bring home the bacon,
but don't be so hi-falootin!
If so, you're good for a laugh or two
(and watch your intake of glutin).

You're full of beans and hot air, too;
and don't try to pull my leg.
So you may as well git!_while the gitins good,
or else for mercy you'll beg!

A lot of baloney we cannot abide,
a real lemon we'll know by the smell.
A monkey's uncle we try not to be:
just go and try another to sell!

Wishes

I know them not. They don't know me,
yet sugary kindness flows.
For when I go to shop or buy,
I meet friendly Janes and Joes.

The clouds may burst with downpour's gray,
the heat may simmer toes.
The cold may numb, the sun may broil
yet some words banish woes.

My purchase made, my duties done,
as I am heading towards the door,
I hear that parting friendly wish
that shakes me to my core.

Some words amuse and light my mood
when hearing someone say
those caring, trite and charming words:
"I hope you have a nice day!"

String Theory

What would we do without guitars,
that instrument of choice,
which accompanies our vocalists
and enhances every voice.

Those strumming and those picking sounds,
and slapping hands on wood,
dominate our recording charts,
making every song sound good.

Sweet songs of love and loss and home
sound great with guitar strings;
and soothe without a yell or scream,
when a talented artist sings.

But the sold-out concerts with rock bands,
with guitars and pounding drum,
combine with screaming fans and star
that leave exposed ears numb.

And let's not speak of acoustic aids
that magnify the sound,
adding further to the din.
It's not where I'll be found!

Forgotten

He stands upon a pedestal,
his name carved into stone,
forgotten although big as life
upon whom once fortune shone.

Pigeons rest upon his head,
fallen leaves in the fall.
He was a hero in his time;
just why I can't recall.

A governor, orator or army general,
his fame deserted now,
reminds us of the moving stage
and the short-lived actor's bow.

The eras pass and take their tales
but leave their heroes here.
I wonder how our own statued names
will puzzle future's peers?

Archive

My little black book is my history parade,
and there could never be a better recorder,
for reviewing my life's journey and recalling what was,
in organized alphabetical order.

From the A's to the Z's my past comes alive,
each letter evokes an old scene:
or a friend long departed with phone number intact.
Just one name is missing : the Queen!

Neighbors we shared fences with and saw every day,
throughout my job-changing past,
to cities and states removed from my roots
are still enshrined as my traveling cast.

So, with every new move and every new job
came additional names to record,
so useful and timely when first carefully noted,
and now striking a familiar chord.

Each name conjures images so long forgotten,
of contacts and sources and places;
like a peek behind curtains that dimmed and hid
my old life's travels and faces.

That little black book is my own life recalled
to dip into for a backward look,
and as a summary of years so swiftly gone by:
as nostalgia and of hands I once shook.

Problems Solved

Elusive perfection blights our days
and eludes without pity
our self-esteem and error-prone pride.

But: man's clever, ingenious and inventive wit
timely salvages our self-inflicted wounds
⋯with correction fluid!

Still More Rambling

There once was a girl called Sadie,
who was anything but a lady;
she was tough and rough,
her voice was gruff,
and she never was afraidy.

Until one day she sassed her mom,
from whom she learned her lessons,
who proved that sass will never pass
without painful woodshed sessions.

There once was a cook named Mark,
who went to the park after dark,
and peeled a tree,
when no one would see,
and tried to make soup out of bark.

He added some juice
from the neck of a goose,
and bone from the tail of a moose;
added pepper and salt,
but didn't know when to halt,
so he threw in the knot of a noose.

The diners went wild, no protests were filed,
the dish became known far and wide.
Other cooks around town
gave Mark a crown,
and stripped every tree of its hide.

Intertwined

Janet is my other half,
my second lung and heart.
If you ask me why that's so,
I don't know where to start!

The years pass by, taking us along,
like free-loaders at a feast;
a bumpy ride, a glitch or two,
memorable, to say the least!

But, at this moment of reflective thought,
her star still illuminates my sky.
She's held my hand and walked with me:
I'm just one lucky guy!

I've known her since our high school days
with backgrounds meshed as one.
Her beauty ripened as we aged,
like flowers in the sun!

She is my buddy and good soul,
through storms and sick and well.
She's joined me with each changing job
and unemployment hell!

She's brought a solid, loving base,
sharing good and ill.
I love my Janet with my remaining strength:
we've shared life's heat and chill!

Words are there to say deep thoughts,
to break through surface murk:
so, here I sit and beg of her,
to please let no doubts lurk!

This poem marks sixty-six married years:
my scrapbook overflows with time.
So, to my sweet Janet, my friend and pal,
I've tried to say "I love you!" in rhyme!

We're tendrils around a solid oak,
intertwined as one;
and if a lightning bolt would hit,
we've had our loving run!

A Toast

Another new year says so long to twelve months,
with sparklers, crazy hats and a horn,
and a twelve o'clock toast with wishes for better
as a new calendar year is born.

Another creak in the bones and a wrinkle or two
keeps pace with the tick of the clock.
We wish for calm seas and a mate that we love,
'til our boat ties up at the dock!

We add up the good things that happened before,
and hope they outnumbered the bad.
We think the same thing year after year,
and wish the happy overshadows the sad.

Final Chores

As the station draws closer, and the clouds slowly darken,
as eerie distant sounds intrude,
ever -assertively, with calendars' passage,
I look at my uneaten food.

It is time to cull, those physical things,
with meaning only to me:
the drawers and shelves, boxes and bins,
like de-nuding a leafy tree.

The endless "one-day-I'll-get-to-its",
those momentos of past jobs and travels,
souvenirs and objects in their dusty niches
will depart as my living unravels.

The carefully hoarded "stuff" which comforted me so,
whose someday use never came,
all cry for reluctant, sorrowful shedding,
some that I hoped would bring fame.

My overflowed closet with suits that don't fit;
sweaters, shirts and ties:
whose comfortable usefulness left long ago
and whose departure would evoke sad sighs.

Reality knocks with increasing persistence
and begs that I minimize the tasks
of those who remain to clean up after.
I tried, if anyone asks!

About the Author

Nathan Polsky, author of three volumes of poetry, *Meaningful Sounds*, *Bountiful Buffet*, and *Traveling Light*, is a native New Yorker. He has been married for over sixty-six years to a woman with whom he attended their high school prom. They have two daughters.

He was an elementary school art teacher, cartoonist, illustrator, fabric designer and artist. His work appeared in various newspapers and periodicals. He won an award from the New York Art Directors Club for a work commissioned by CBS. He is still a working artist.

During World War II, he was a bombardier, flying over two dozen missions, earning a Purple Heart and two Bronze Stars.

Polsky has a BS and an MA degree from NYU. His professional career included being Director of several community arts organizations, Project Director at Macmillan and Houghton Mifflin publishers, and advertising manager with several paper companies.

He founded and was president of Scratch-Art Co., an arts and crafts company, inventing and manufacturing many original creative art products for schools and commercial markets before finally selling the company and retiring.

For the last several years, he has concentrated on writing poems, focusing on personal thoughts, observations, experiences, memories, etc. seeing the serious and humorous sides of life.

Previously Published By Nathan Polsky

MEANINGFUL SOUNDS: New and Collected Poems, Vol. 1

© 2013, Nathan Polsky

BOUNTIFUL BUFFET: New and Collected Poems, Vol. 2

© 2013, Nathan Polsky

TRAVELING LIGHT: New and Collected Poems, Vol. 3

© 2014, Nathan Polsky

Available at Barnes & Noble online and Amazon.com
(eBook and Paperback versions)

Also available at the Village Voices book shop in Bradenton, FL, and other independent booksellers.

Suncoast Digital Press, Inc. is a publishing company in Sarasota, Florida. For more information on this author or other books published by Suncoast Digital Press, Inc., visit

www.SuncoastDigitalPress.com.

www.ingramcontent.com/pod-product-compliance
Lightning Source LLC
Chambersburg PA
CBHW070642050426

42451CB00008B/265